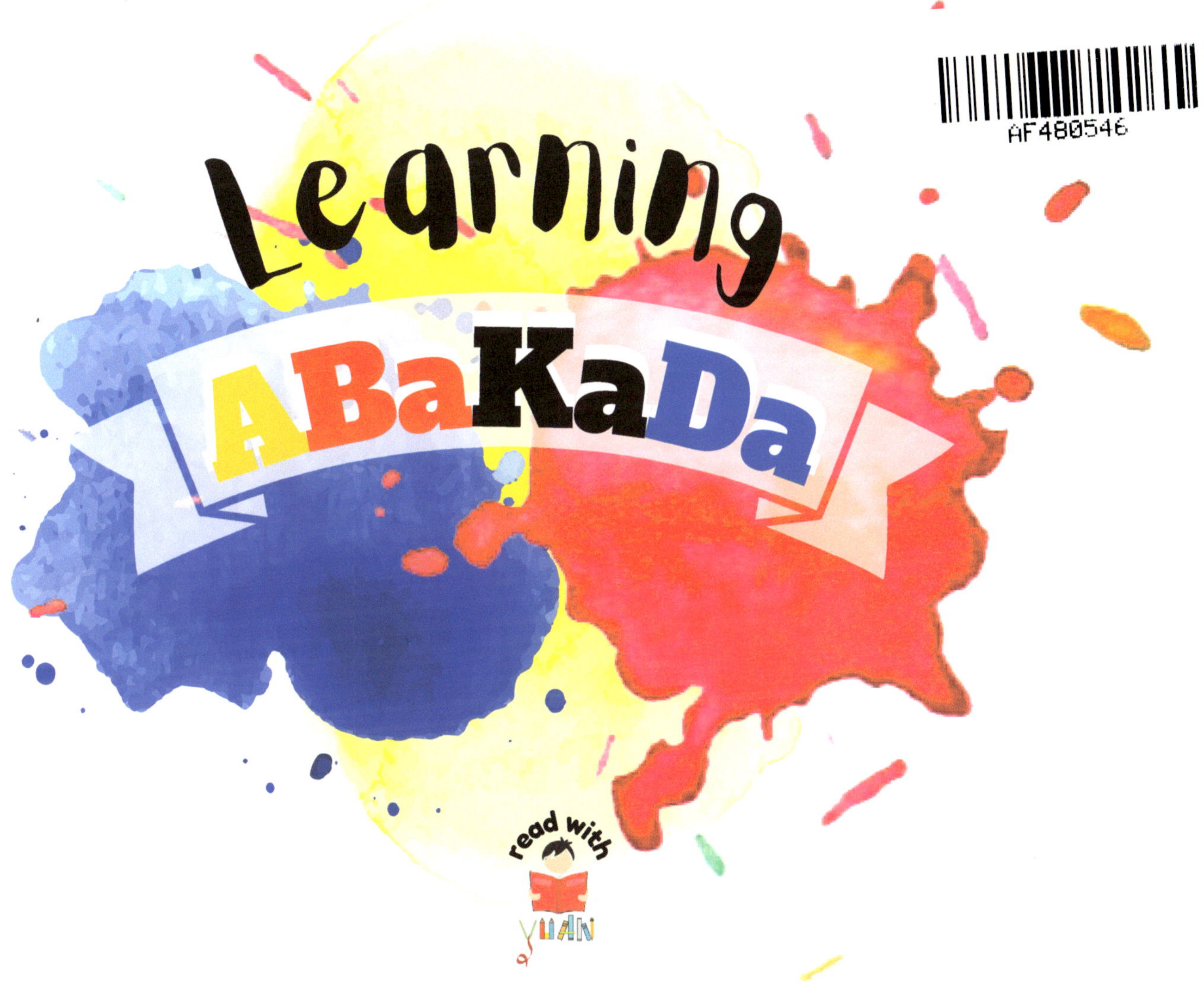

Learning ABaKaDa

Learn and explore the Philippines' native alphabet ABaKaDa with this fun and colorful book.

Aa
(ah)
aso
(ah-so)
dog
abokado
(ah-bo-kah-do)
avocado
ahas
(ah-has)
snake
aklat
(ahk-lat)
book
apoy
(ah-poy)
fire
araw
(ah-raw)
sun
apat
(ah-pat)
four

6

anim
(ah-neem)
six

agila
(ah-gee-la)
eagle

alkansiya
(ahl-kan-sha)
piggybank

alon
(ah-lon)
wave

ampalaya
(ahm-pah-lah-yah)
bittermelon

alahas
(ah-lah-has)
jewelry

Bb
(ba)

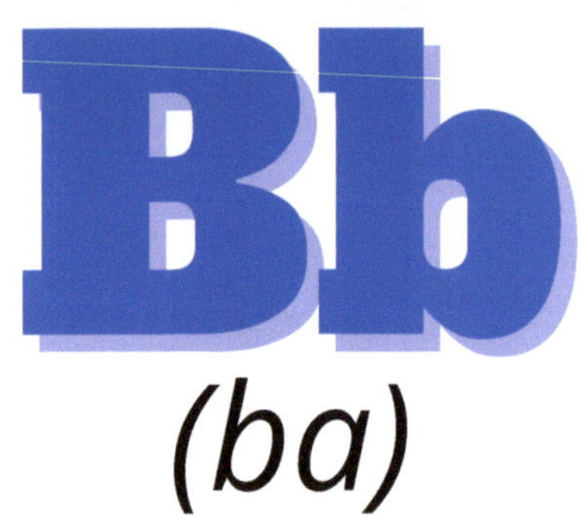

baso
(bah-so)
glass

bintana
(been-tah-nah)
window

baboy
(bah-boy)
pig

bahay
(bah-hay)
house

bola
(boh-lah)
ball

butiki
(boo-tee-kee)
lizard

buwan
(boo-whan)
moon

bahaghari
(bah-hag-hah-ree)
rainbow

bundok
(boon-dok)
mountain

buhok
(boo-hook)
hair

baka
(bah-kah)
cow

bulaklak
(boo-lhak-lhak)
flower

bawang
(bah-whang)
garlic

Kk
(ka)

kahon
(kah-hon)
box

kabayo
(kah-bah-yo)
horse

keso
(keh-so)
cheese

kamay
(kah-mhay)
hand

kalabasa
(kah-lah-bah-sah)
squash

kawal
(kah-wal)
knight

kalan
(kah-lan)
stove

kutsilyo
(koot-sil-yo)
knife

kadena
(kah-deh-nah)
chain

kuneho
(koo-ne-ho)
bunny

kalabaw
(kah-lah-bow)
water buffalo

kambing
(kham-bing)
goat

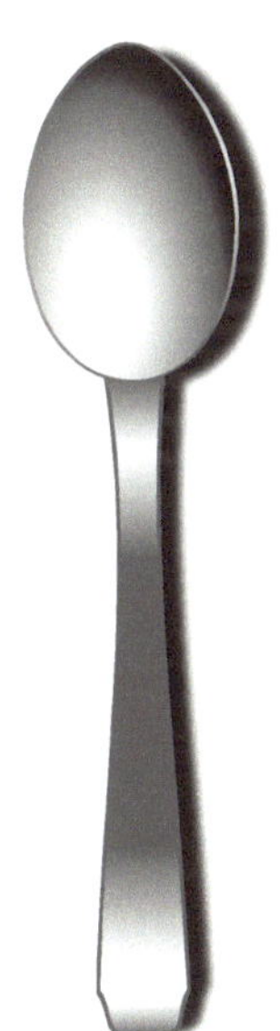

kutsara
(koot-sah-rah)
spoon

kotse
(khot-che)
car

Dd
(da)

dyamante
(ja-mhan-te)
diamond

diyaryo
(jar-yo)
newspaper

dahon
(dah-hon)
leaf

diwata
(dee-wah-tah)
fairy

dalandan
(dah-lhan-dhan)
orange

damit
(dah-meet)
clothes

damo
(dah-moh)
grass

dagat
(dah-gat)
sea

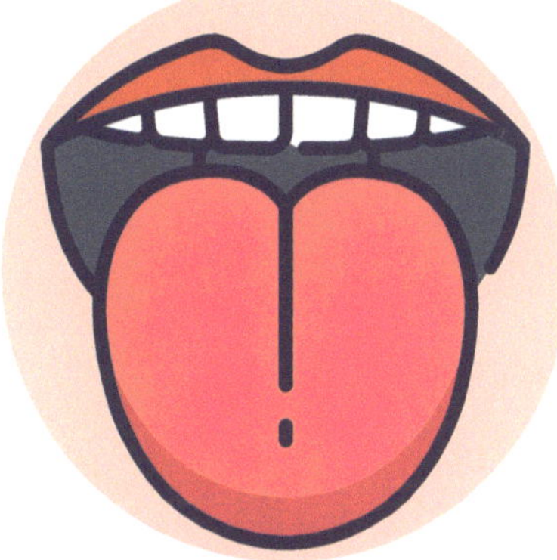

dila
(dee-lah)
tongue

doktor
(dok-tor)
doctor

dalawa
(dah-lah-wah)
two

daga
(dah-ga)
rat

daigdig
(dah-ig-dig)
world

Ee
(eh)

espada
(es-pah-dah)
sword

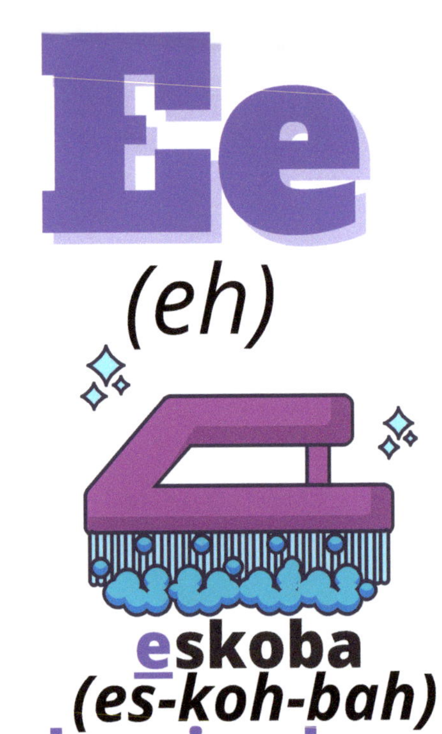

eskoba
(es-koh-bah)
cleaning brush

eroplano
(eh-ro-plah-noh)
airplane

eskinita
(es-ki-nee-tah)
alley

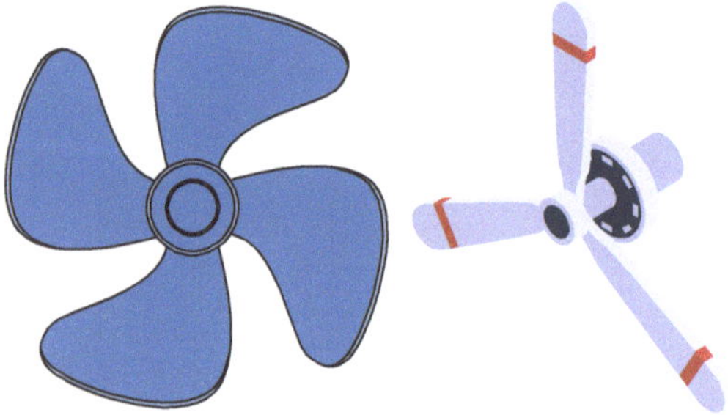

elisi
(eh-li-see)
propeller

estatwa
(es-tat-wah)
statue

elepante
(e-le-pan-teh)
elephant
embudo
(em-boo-doh)
funnel
eskwelahan
(es-kwe-lah-han)
school
estudyante
(es-too-jan-teh)
student
espongha
(es-pong-ha)
sponge
ehersisyo
(eh-her-sis-yo)
exercise

Gg
(ga)

gatas
(gah-tas)
milk

gulong
(goo-long)
tire

gansa
(ghan-sah)
goose

ginto
(geen-to)
gold

garapon
(gah-rah-pon)
jar

globo
(glo-boh)
globe

gantsilyo
(ghan-sil-yo)
crochet

gamot
(gah-mot)
medicine

gunting
(goon-ting)
scissors

gatong
(gah-tong)
firewood

faucet

gripo
(gree-po)

gabi
(gah-bee)
night

gadgaran
(ghad-gah-ran)
grater

gagamba
(gah-gam-bah)
spider

gitara
(gee-tah-rah)
guitar

Hh
(ha)

hangin
(ha-ngeen)
wind

hagdan
(hag-dan)
ladder

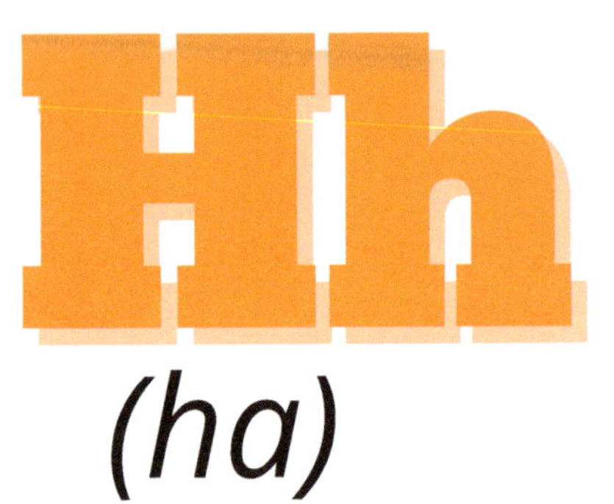

halaman
(ha-lah-man)
plant

hardin
(har-deen)
garden

habilog
(ha-bee-log)
oval

hinlalaki
(heen-lah-lah-key)
thumb

hipon
(hee-pon)
shrimp

hawla
(how-lah)
cage

h̲ikab
(hee-cab)
yawn

h̲alik
(ha-leek)
kiss

h̲olen
(ho-len)
marble

h̲atsing
(hat-ching)
sneeze

h̲ikaw
(hee-cow)
earrings

h̲amon
(ha-mon)
ham

h̲ari
(ha-ree)
king

Ii
(ih)

ilaw
(ee-law)
light

itlog
(eet-log)
egg

igat
(ee-gat)
eel

isla
(ees-lah)
island

isa
(ee-sah)
one

ibon
(ee-bon)
bird

ipis
(ee-pees)
cockroach

isda
(ees-dah)
fish

ina
(ee-nah)
mother

iyak
(ee-yak)
cry

inom
(ee-nom)
drink

ilog
(ee-log)
river

itim
(ee-team)
black

ihaw
(ee-how)
grill

itik
(ee-tik)
brown duck

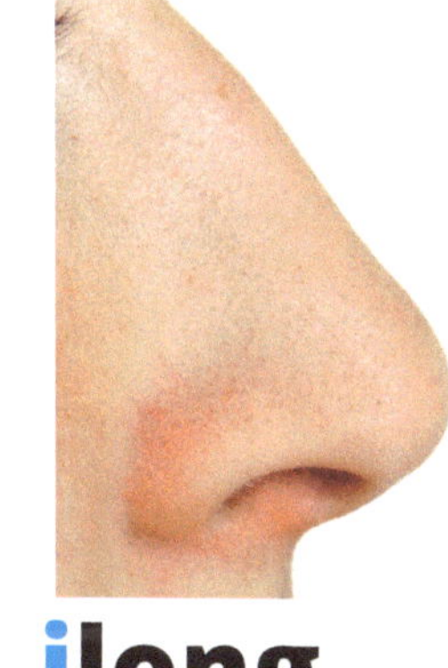

ilong
(ee-long)
nose

Ll
(la)

lata
(lah-tah)
tin can

lola
(loh-lah)
grandma

lolo
(loh-loh)
grandpa

lalaki
(lah-lah-kee)
male

libro
(leeb-roh)
book

5
lima
(lee-mah)
five

lamesa
(lah-meh-sah)
table

larawan
(lah-rah-wan)
picture

lampin
(lham-pin)
diaper

lapis
(lah-peas)
pencil

langaw
(lah-ngaw)
fly

lagari
(lah-ga-ree)
saw

leon
(lee-yawn)
lion

langgam
(lhang-gum)
ant

ligo
(lee-go)
shower

lamok
(lah-mok)
mosquito

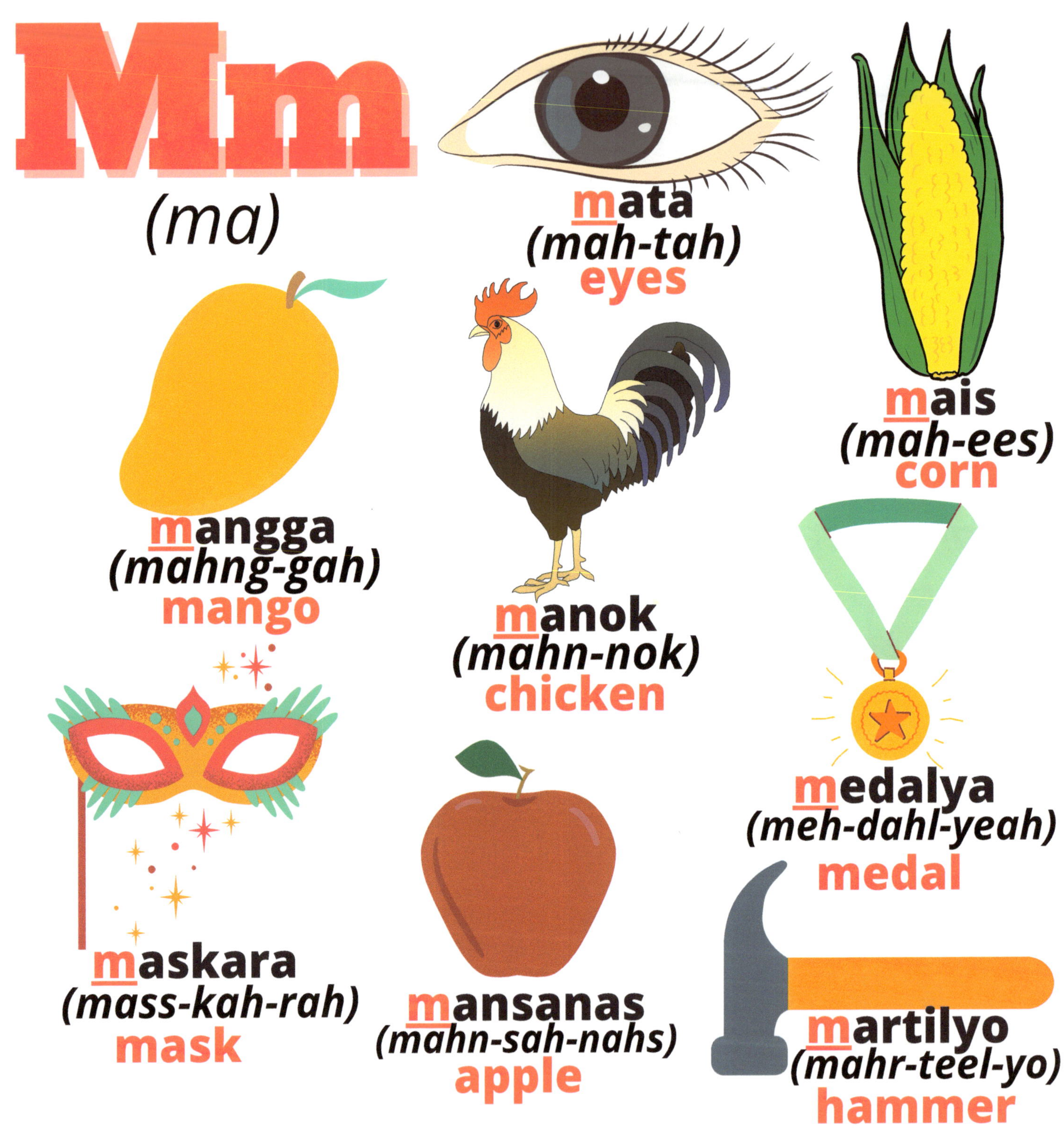

Mm
(ma)
mata
(mah-tah)
eyes
mais
(mah-ees)
corn
mangga
(mahng-gah)
mango
manok
(mahn-nok)
chicken
medalya
(meh-dahl-yeah)
medal
maskara
(mass-kah-rah)
mask
mansanas
(mahn-sah-nahs)
apple
martilyo
(mahr-teel-yo)
hammer

medida
(meh-dee-dah)
tape measure

manika
(mahn-nee-kah)
doll

mamon
(mah-mon)
sponge cake

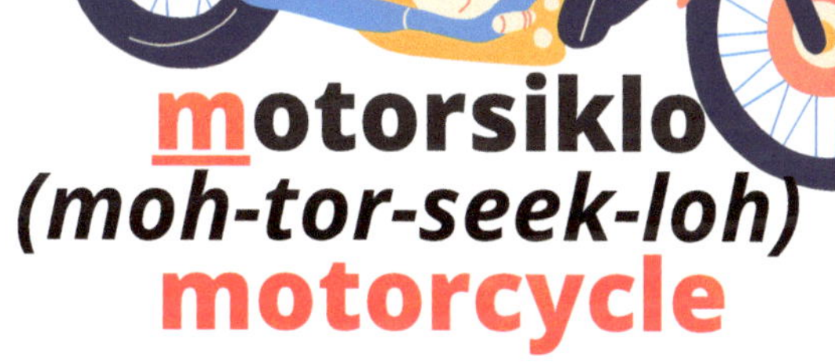

motorsiklo
(moh-tor-seek-loh)
motorcycle

mantika
(mahn-tee-kah)
cooking oil

medyas
(med-yahs)
socks

mani
(mahn-nee)
peanut

Nn
(na)

niyog
(nee-yog)
coconut

nota
(noh-tah)
music notes

norte
(nor-teh)
north

nyebe
(knee-ye-beh)
snow

nipa
(nee-pah)
nipa palm

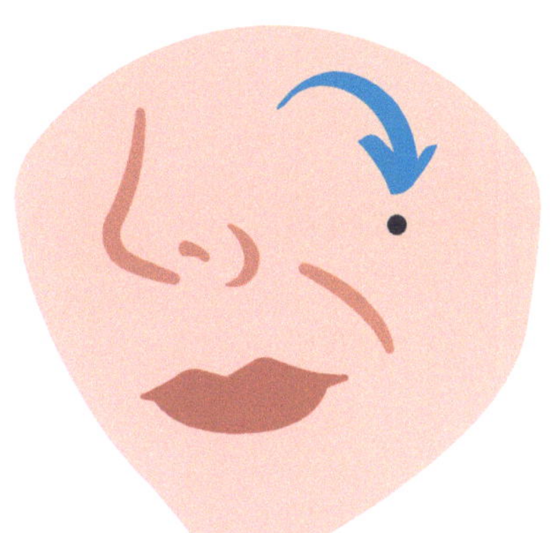

nunal
(noo-nahl)
mole

nars
(nahrs)
nurse

nayon
(nah-yon)
village

numero
(noh-me-roh)
number

noo
(noh-o)
forehead

Ng

(nga)

<u>ng</u>uso
(ngoo-so)
snout

<u>ng</u>anga
(ngah-ngah)
mouth open

<u>ng</u>iti
(ngee-tee)
smile

<u>ng</u>inig
(ngee-neeg)
shiver

<u>ng</u>ipin
(ngee-pin)
teeth

Oo
(oh)

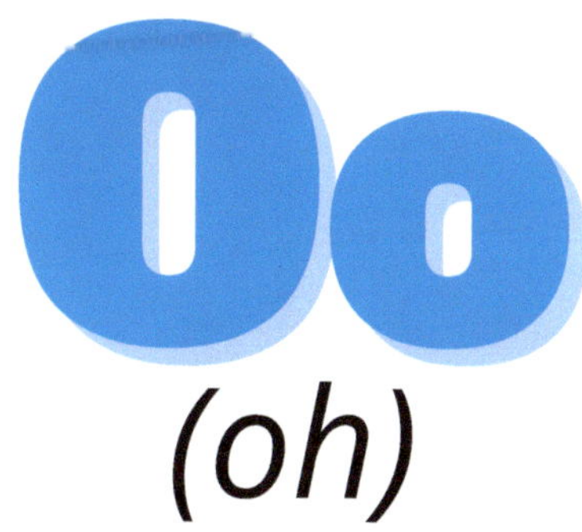

orasan
(oh-rah-sun
clock

oras
(oh-rahs)
time

ohales
(oh-ha-less)
buttonhole

oktubre
(ok-toob-re)
october

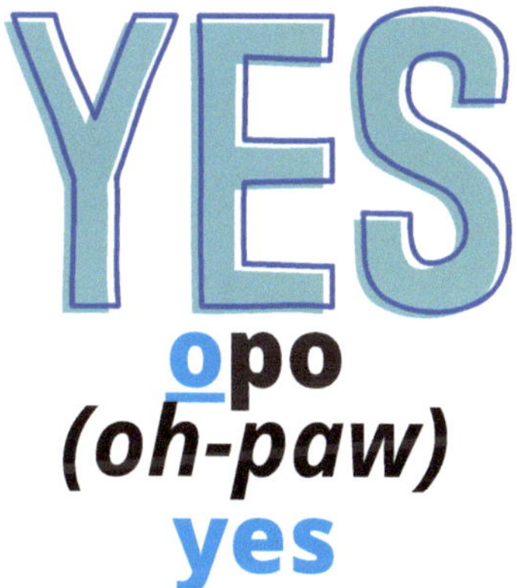

opo
(oh-paw)
yes

oso
(oh-saw)
bear

ospital
(os-pee-tahl)
hospital

P p
(pa)

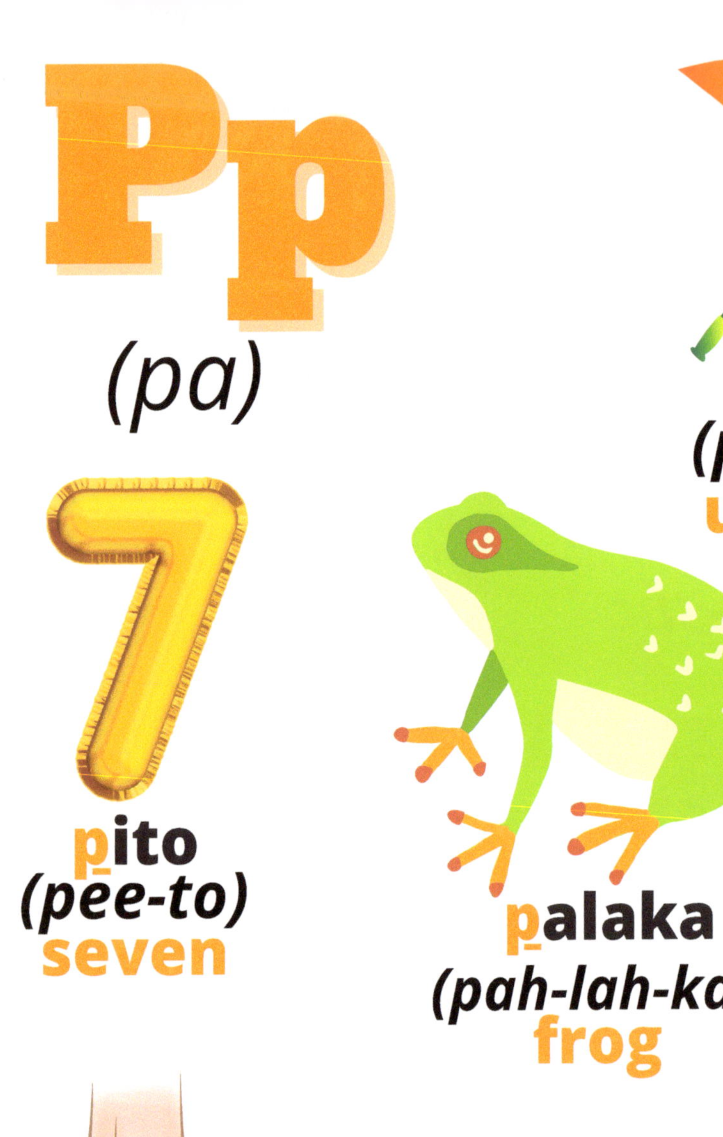

pito
(pee-to)
seven

palaka
(pah-lah-kah)
frog

payong
(pah-yong)
umbrella

pinya
(pin-yeah)
pineapple

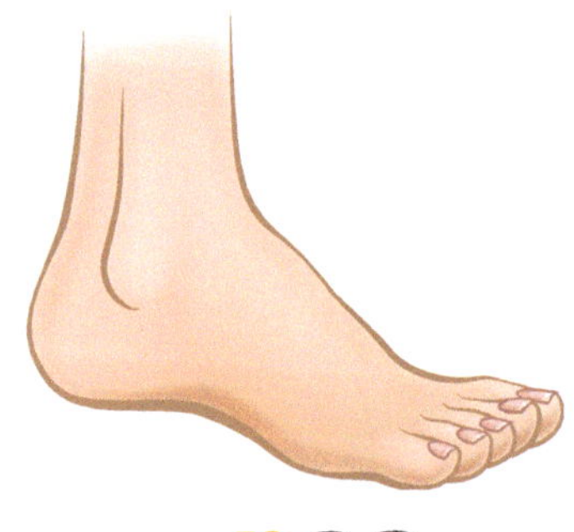

paa
(pah-ah)
foot

pusa
(poo-sah)
cat

pako
(pah-koh)
nail

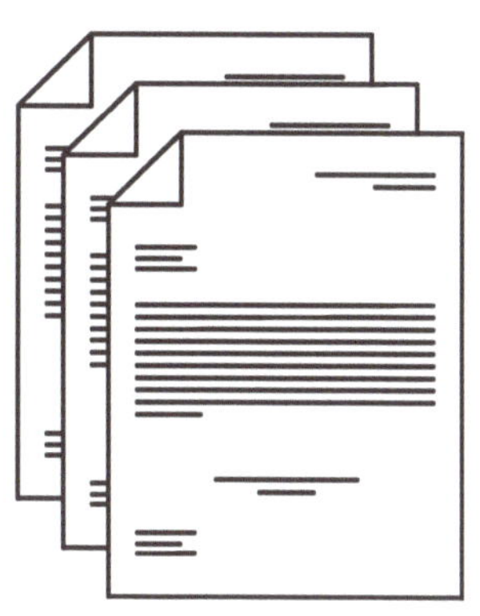

p̲apel
(pah-pel)
paper

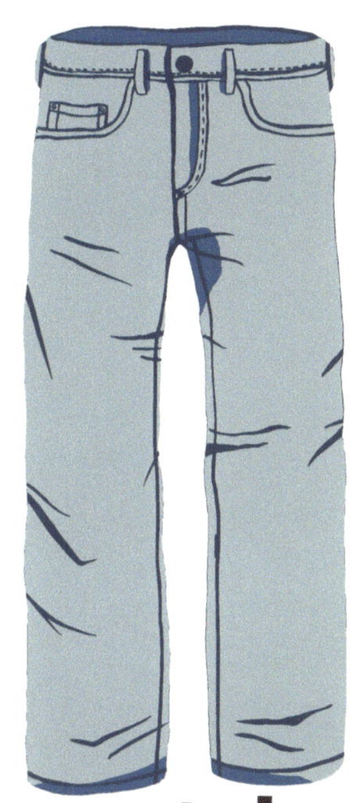

p̲antalon
(pahn-tah-lon)
pants

p̲aruparo
(pah-roh-pah-roh)
butterfly

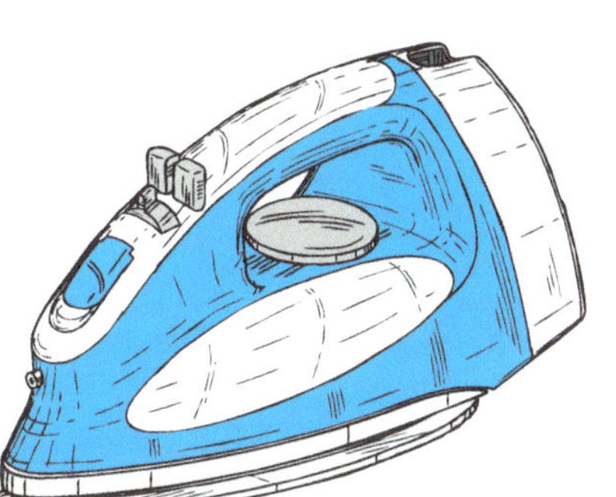

p̲lantsa
(plan-cha)
iron

p̲itsel
(peet-chel)
pitcher

p̲abo
(pah-bo)
turkey

p̲uno
(puh-noh)
tree

Rr
(ra)

rosaryo
(roh-sar-yo)
rosary

rosas
(roh-sas)
rose

relo
(reh-loh)
watch

reyna
(ray-nah)
queen

regalo
(reh-gah-lo)
gift

radyo
(rad-yo)
radio

roleta
(roh-leh-tah)
roulette

raketa
(rah-keh-tah)
racket

riles
(ree-less)
railway

resibo
(reh-see-bo)
receipt

repolyo
(reh-pol-yo)
cabbage

repriherador
(rep-ree-hee-rah-dor)
refrigerator

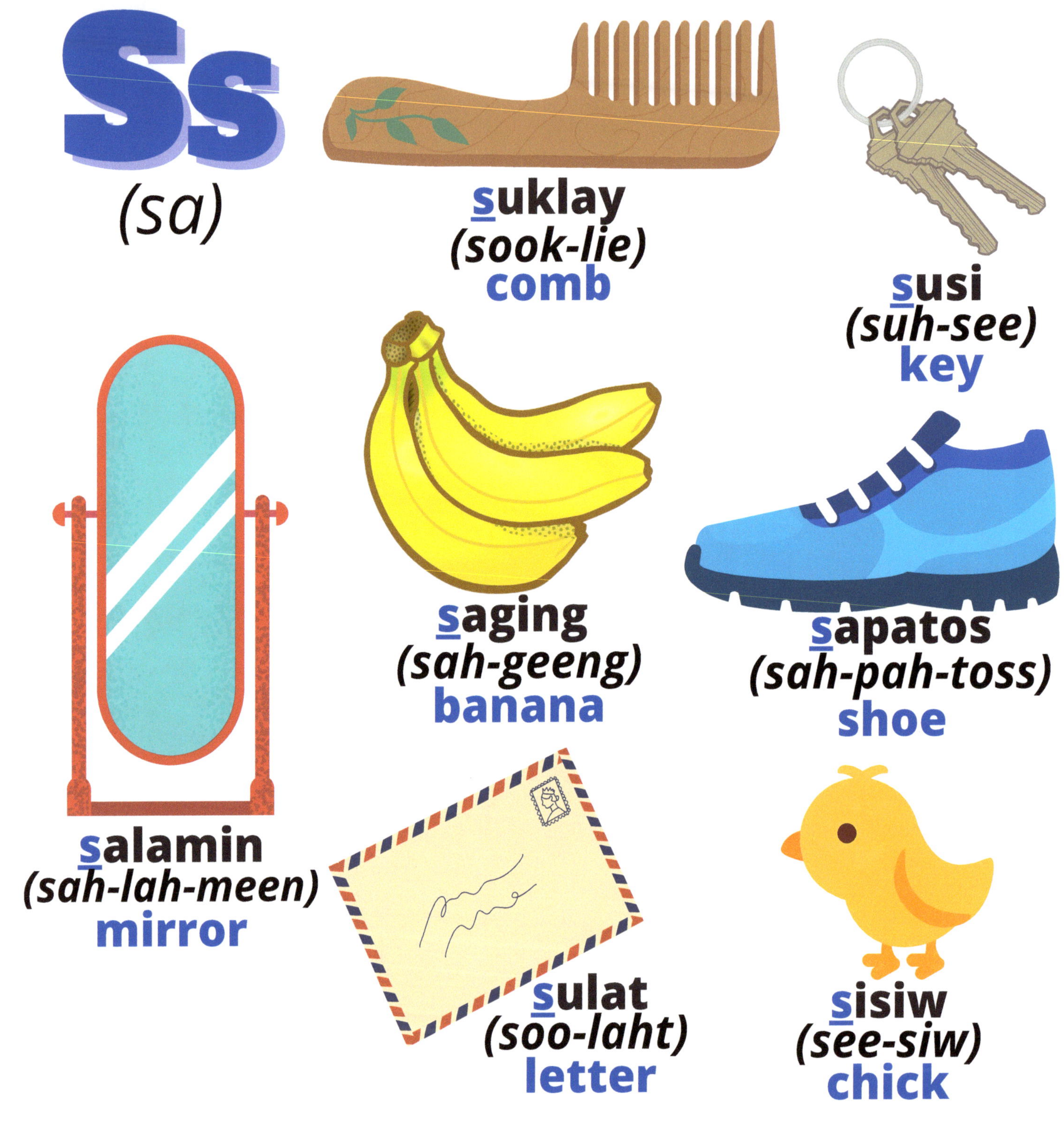

Ss
(sa)
suklay
(sook-lie)
comb
susi
(suh-see)
key
saging
(sah-geeng)
banana
sapatos
(sah-pah-toss)
shoe
salamin
(sah-lah-meen)
mirror
sulat
(soo-laht)
letter
sisiw
(see-siw)
chick

sayaw
(sah-yaw)
dance

sabon
(sah-bohn)
soap

sombrero
(som-bre-roh)
hat

sahig
(sah-heeg)
floor

sandok
(san-dok)
laddle

sipilyo
(see-pil-yo)
toothbrush

sasakyan
(sah-sak-yan)
car

sabaw
(sah-baw)
soup

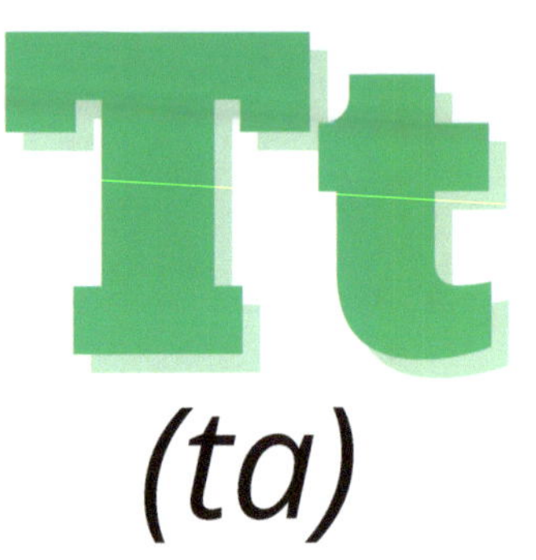

Tt
(ta)

t̲inidor
(tee-nee-dor)
fork

t̲atlo
(tat-loh)
three

t̲atsulok
(tat-soo-look)
triangle

t̲asa
(tah-sah)
cup

t̲ali
(tah-lee)
string

t̲abo
(tah-boh)
water dipper

t̲inapay
(tee-nah-pie)
bread

t̲ala
(tah-lah)
star

t̲sinelas
(chi-ne-las)
slippers

t̲uwalya
(to-wahl-yah)
towel

t̲akip
(tah-keep)
cover

t̲uta
(too-tah)
puppy

t̲igre
(teeg-ree)
tiger

t̲akbo
(tak-boh)
run

t̲upa
(too-pah)
sheep

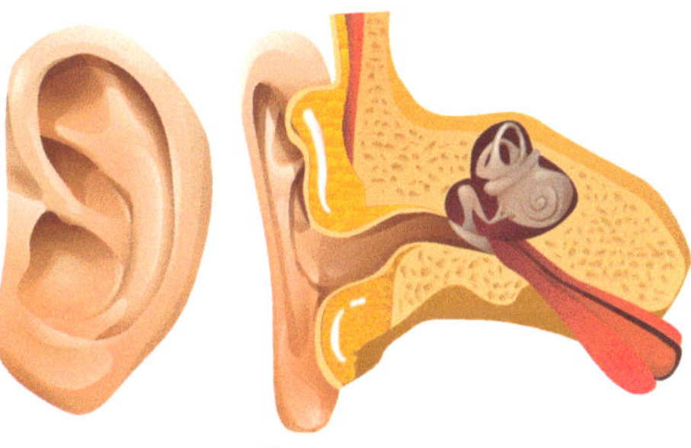

t̲ainga
(teh-nga)
ear

Uu

(uh)

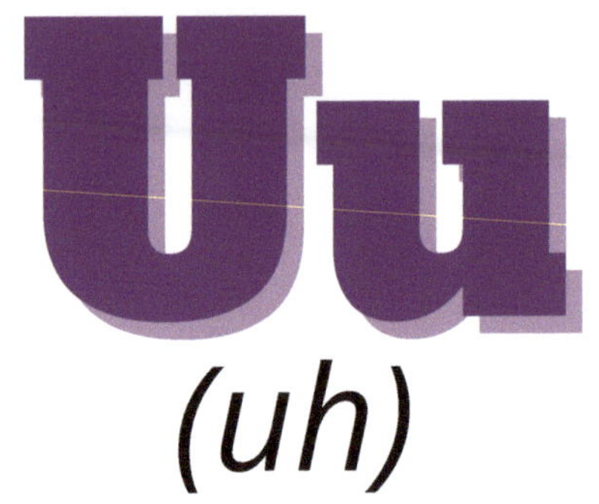

ubas
(oo-bass)
grapes

ugat
(oo-gat)
roots

ulan
(oo-lan)
rain

unan
(oo-nan)
pillow

ube
(oo-be)
purple yam

uod
(oo-ud)
worm

utak
(oo-tak)
brain

umaga
(oo-mah-gah)
morning

ulang
(oo-lahng)
crayfish

ulap
(oo-lap)
cloud

ulo
(oo-lo)
head

usok
(oo-sok)
smoke

Ww
(wa)

w̲asak
(wah-sak)
destroy

w̲atawat
(wah-tah-what)
flag

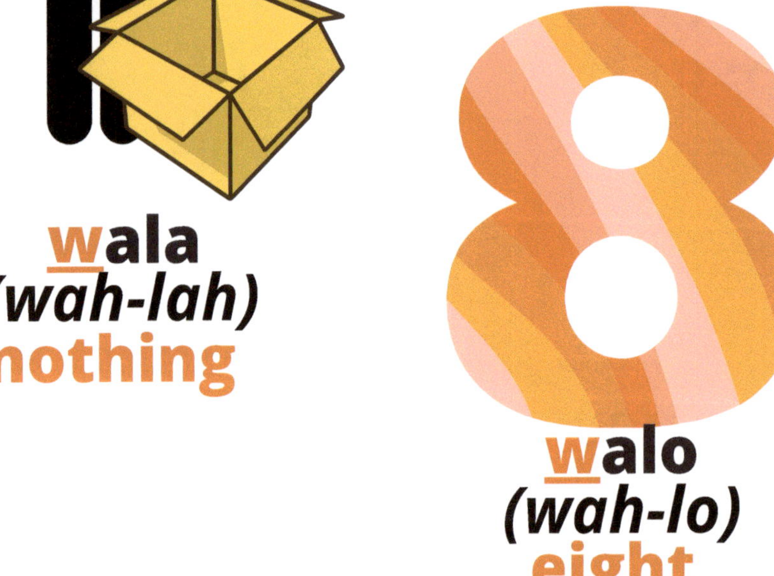

w̲ala
(wah-lah)
nothing

w̲alo
(wah-lo)
eight

w̲alis
(wah-lis)
broom

Yy
(ya)

y.apak
(yah-pak)
footprint

y.akap
(yah-kap)
hug

y.ungib
(yoh-ngeeb)
cave

y.elo
(yeah-lo)
ice

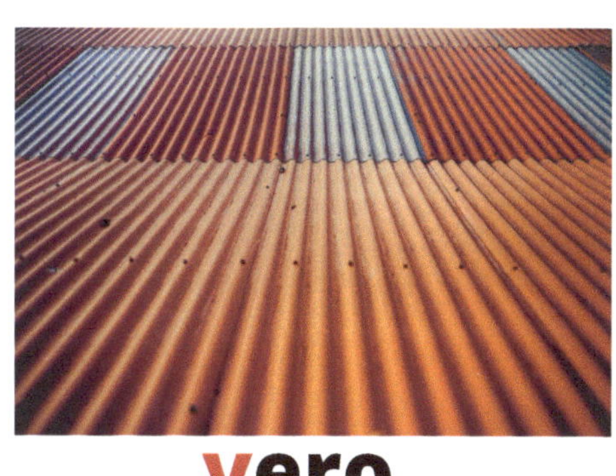

y.ero
(yeah-ro)
metal roof

y.upi
(yoo-pee)
dent

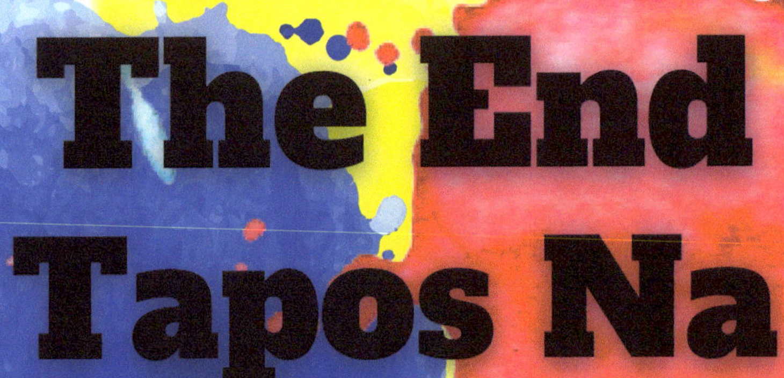

The End
Tapos Na